Judy Blume

WHO
WROTE
THAT?

Judy Blume

Elisa Ludwig

Foreword by
Kyle Zimmer

Chelsea House Publishers
Philadelphia

CHELSEA HOUSE PUBLISHERS

VP, NEW PRODUCT DEVELOPMENT Sally Cheney
DIRECTOR OF PRODUCTION Kim Shinners
CREATIVE MANAGER Takeshi Takahashi
MANUFACTURING MANAGER Diann Grasse

STAFF FOR JUDY BLUME

EDITOR Benjamin Kim
PICTURE RESEARCHER Pat Holl
PRODUCTION EDITOR Megan Emery
SERIES DESIGNER Keith Trego
LAYOUT 21st Century Publishing and Communications, Inc.

http://www.chelseahouse.com

First Printing

1 3 5 7 9 8 6 4 2

Library of Congress Cataloging-in-Publication Data

Ludwig, Elisa.
  Judy Blume / by Elisa Ludwig.
     p. cm. — (Who wrote that?)
  Includes index.
  Summary: A biography of Judy Blume, author of a number of popular and
controversial books for young people.
  ISBN 0-7910-7619-9
  1. Blume, Judy—Juvenile literature. 2. Authors, American—20th
century—Biography—Juvenile literature. 3. Children's stories—
Authorship—Juvenile literature. [1. Blume, Judy. 2. Authors, American.
3. Women—Biography.] I. Title. II. Series. PS3552.L843 Z77 2003
813'.54—dc22

                                                2003019352

Table of Contents

FOREWORD BY
KYLE ZIMMER
PRESIDENT, FIRST BOOK

HUMANITY IS POWERED by stories. From our earliest days as thinking beings, we employed every available tool to tell each other stories. We danced, drew pictures on the walls of our caves, spoke, and sang. All of this extraordinary effort was designed to entertain, recount the news of the day, explain natural occurrences—and then gradually to build religious and cultural traditions and establish the common bonds and continuity that eventually formed civilizations. Stories are the most powerful force in the universe; they are the primary element that has distinguished our evolutionary path.

Our love of the story has not diminished with time. Enormous segments of societies are devoted to the art of storytelling. Book sales in the United States alone topped $26 billion last year; movie studios spend fortunes to create and promote stories; and the news industry is more pervasive in its presence than ever before.

There is no mystery to our fascination. Great stories are magic. They can introduce us to new cultures, or remind us of the nobility and failures of our own, inspire us to greatness or scare us to death; but above all, stories provide human insight on a level that is unavailable through any other source. In fact, stories connect each of us to the rest of humanity not just in our own time, but also throughout history.

This special magic of books is the greatest treasure that we can hand down from generation to generation. In fact, that spark in a child that comes from books became the motivation for the creation of my organization, First Book, a national literacy program with a simple mission: to provide new books to the most disadvantaged children. At present, First Book has been at work in hundreds of communities for over a decade. Every year children in need receive millions of books through our organization and millions more are provided through dedicated literacy institutions across the United States and around the world. In addition, groups of people dedicate themselves tirelessly to working with children to share reading and stories in every imaginable setting from schools to the streets. Of course, this Herculean effort serves many important goals. Literacy translates to productivity and employability in life and many other valid and even essential elements. But at the heart of this movement are people who love stories, love to read and want desperately to ensure that no one misses the wonderful possibilities that reading provides.

When thinking about the importance of books, there is an overwhelming urge to cite the literary devotion of great minds. Some have written of the magnitude of the importance of literature. Amy Lowell, an American poet, captured the concept with her statement when she said, "Books are more than books. They are the life, the very heart and core of ages past, the reason why men lived and worked and died, the essence and quintessence of their lives." Others have spoken of their personal obsession with books, as in Thomas Jefferson's simple statement: "I live for books." But more compelling, perhaps, is the almost instinctive excitement in children for books and stories.

Throughout my years at First Book, I have heard truly extraordinary stories about the power of books in the lives of children. In one case, a homeless child, who had been bounced from one location to another, later resurfaced—and the only possession that he had fought to keep was the book he was given as part of a First Book distribution months earlier. More recently, I met a child who, upon receiving the book he wanted, flashed a big smile and said, "This is my big chance!" These snapshots reveal the true power of books and stories to give hope and change lives.

As these children grow up and continue to develop their love of reading, they will owe a profound debt to those volunteers who reached out to them—a debt that they may repay by reaching out to spark the next generation of readers. But there is a greater debt owed by all of us—a debt to the storytellers, the authors, who have bound us together, inspired our leaders, fueled our civilizations, and helped us put our children to sleep with their heads full of images and ideas.

WHO WROTE THAT? is a series of books dedicated to introducing us to a few of these incredible individuals. While we have almost always honored stories, we have not uniformly honored storytellers. In fact, some of the most important authors have toiled in complete obscurity throughout their lives or have been openly persecuted for the uncomfortable truths that they have laid before us. When confronted with the magnitude of their written work or perhaps the daily grind of our own, we can forget that writers are people. They struggle through the same daily indignities and dental appointments, and they experience the intense joy and bottomless despair that many of us do. Yet somehow they rise above it all to deliver a powerful thread that connects us all. It is a rare honor to have the opportunity that these books provide to share the lives of these extraordinary people. Enjoy.

Judy Blume wasn't always a famous writer. As a housewife and mother embarking on a writing career in the 1960s, her early efforts met with many rejections and setbacks. Fortunately for her readers, she never lost faith, and today she is perhaps the world's best-known author of young-adult fiction.

1

Otherwise Known as Judy the Great

Writing changed my life forever. It may have even saved it. [1]
—Judy Blume

JUDY BLUME FINISHED doing the dishes and sat down at her old college typewriter. Her children had been washed, changed, and put to bed. It was in these evening hours that she had a small window of time alone. Now it was time to try and capture the story she had been telling to herself, to see if she could get it right on the page. She was focused, and she began to write, letting the words in her head flow out through her fingertips. Occasionally she would check the notebook she

11

kept on her desk, in which she had scribbled notes and jotted down thoughts about her story during the day.

It was the late 1960s. While other young people had become involved with countercultural movements like the protest against the Vietnam War, the twenty-five-year-old Blume was married and had two children. Judy and her husband John Blume, their son Larry, and their daughter Randy were living in suburban New Jersey. Like many middle-class people at the time, John worked while Judy stayed at home with the children.

Judy Blume loved her children and loved spending time with them. Lately, though, Judy had begun to feel that something was missing from her life. She had always been told that she would grow up, get married, and have children, and that any career plans she might have would be a backup—that is, in case she didn't find a husband to support her. What she was finding, though, after a few years of marriage was that she enjoyed raising a family and doing housework; but it was not completely fulfilling. What she needed was a creative outlet to keep her mind occupied.

She remembered how much she had enjoyed telling stories as a child. Lately she found herself rhyming stories while cleaning up the kitchen and doing other household chores. Larry and Randy were now in preschool, which gave her some time to sit down and sketch out her ideas on pieces of paper. Late at night she would develop her ideas into stories, typing them out on her old college typewriter. She began writing as a hobby, but she started to wish for more. If she could get her books published, she might be able to make a career out of writing. The thought was exciting but the reality was still elusive—she had written two picture books for children but no one wanted to publish them.

It would take persistence and determination for Blume to become a published author. Like many young writers, she faced rejection, both from publishers and people she knew. When she mentioned what she was working on, people scoffed at her dream and told her she was not a "real" writer. They would try to discourage her by asking, "What makes you think you can write?" A friend of her husband's who had been an English major in college told her, "You're a nice girl, Judy, but you can't write."

At first these comments hurt her, but over time she learned to ignore the people who doubted her and focused on her work instead. For two years she would send her writing to publishing houses only to get rejection slips in return. *Highlights Magazine for Children* sent her back a form rejection letter that contained a checklist with the reason, "Does not win in competition with others" checked off. This was puzzling and painful, but Blume got used to the rejections and kept working. She kept telling herself that someone, somewhere would want to read her stories. Every night she would go to sleep feeling the sting of criticism and wondering if she would ever be published. But every morning she would wake up with new-found optimism and start working on a new story.

When she was twenty-seven, Blume got a brochure in the mail from New York University that advertised a class on writing for children. She recalls, "I was already trying to do picture books, so I considered the brochure an omen. I signed up for that class and took a bus from New Jersey into the city one evening a week." [2]

The course at NYU turned out to be quite a boon to

Blume's career. Her teacher, Lee Wyndham, praised her work and encouraged her to continue. Wyndham herself had written over fifty books and hundreds of short stories, and was considered an expert in children's literature. With Wyndham's encouragement, Blume worked diligently and quickly, churning out pages of new material each week. When the class ended after a semester, she signed up and took it again the next.

All the practice in class paid off—before the second semester ended, Blume found out that a few of her stories were accepted for publication in a magazine. She was paid only twenty dollars for the stories, but the idea of finally getting her stories published was very exciting. Wyndham gave her a red rose in class to congratulate her.

Blume knew then that she was going to be a writer. She still didn't know much about writing or what to expect, and she certainly had no big plan for her books to become best-sellers. She didn't worry about pleasing adults or even becoming a revered children's author. All she wanted to do was to write the kinds of books she herself would have wanted to read when she was younger.

A lifelong reader, Blume had loved stories of all kinds when she was a child. But no matter how much she read, she never found characters in those stories who resembled her. Real life, which was full of worries, frustrations, and embarrassing moments, was strangely absent in the books of her youth. In that era, children's books presented only one kind of world, where the illustrations were bright and colorful and the children in them always looked perfect. There were never images of people of color, people with disabilities, or families with problems. The stories themselves told about happy times and gave children instructions on how to do things the right way, which always seemed hopelessly simplistic. For Judy Blume, they did not ring true.

"When I was a kid," she told CBS radio's Don Swaim in 1984, "I couldn't find satisfaction in children's books. I couldn't find myself in them, my thoughts and feelings and fears."

She decided that her own books would address what no one else had written about. Just because a child was only ten years old, she reasoned, did not mean that he or she didn't have problems. In fact, it was often the case that children's problems seemed more threatening because the child felt alone and the cheerful, unrealistic books they were reading made them feel even lonelier. Blume was sure that there was also room for stories about different kinds of children, living under different kinds of circumstances. Kids were often under the control of their parents and forced to accept the decisions their parents made. Blume wanted to write books that addressed the helplessness and frustration kids can feel, as well as their fears. Being young when things seem new and mysterious is bad enough, but adults rarely revealed the truth to their children. Blume also wanted to write about the kinds of things that kids feared most but were least explained by adults.

Blume could remember her own fears while growing up. In fact, she found that once she thought about it, she could remember the entire experience of childhood, which brought her closer to the characters she was creating. While sitting down to write her earliest books for children, she found that she could effortlessly slip into her own childhood memories and capture the feelings of her past, then turn them into words on the page.

After her first few stories were published, Blume devoted her time in class to writing her first novel,

Blume's first novel, Iggie's House, *reflected the racial tensions of the 1960s, when African Americans struggled for civil rights. In the story, young people are forced to face the adult problems of discrimination that confronted the nation. Blume's work would continue to break down barriers, addressing new and controversial topics for young audiences.*

Iggie's House. The novel was about some of the racial tensions Blume saw around her at that time when African-American people were fighting for civil rights. The reaction among white people in the suburbs was fear and racism. People she knew talked about arming themselves in case the riots that were taking place in Newark, New Jersey, happened to spill over into their suburban neighborhood.

Blume found their response disturbing and decided to write about it. In the book, an African-American family moves into a white suburban neighborhood and faces similar discrimination. The book was also about how a young white girl who befriends her new neighbors tries to understand what is going on. The book was typical of Judy Blume's work in that it captured the confusion of being young and yet having to face adult problems.

The book was written rather quickly. Blume turned in a chapter a week to Lee Wyndham who would praise her work and offer her constructive criticism. When she had completed the manuscript of *Iggie's House*, Blume decided to send it to an editor she had read about in *Writer's Digest* magazine. His name was Dick Jackson and he was known for taking new authors under his wing. Blume hoped that he would agree to meet with her and help publish her book.

In the meantime, she had learned that her picture book, *The One in the Middle Is the Green Kangaroo*, was going to be published. She was ecstatic, and she described her reaction to her biographer Maryann Weidt:

> The children, then about five and seven years old, were in the basement playing with something called Silly Sand. It was like dried pieces of balsa wood. You soaked it in water and then you could mold it. It was very messy stuff. When they called to offer me the contract, I was so excited, I ran down the stairs and put my hands into this bowl of Silly Sand and threw it all over the place. Then I picked up the kids and spun them around. Laurie Murphy, Larry's best friend, looked at me and left, crying. She went home and told her mother that Larry's mother had gone crazy. [3]

It was the last time she would throw art materials

around, but it was not the last time she would hear such good news. Shortly afterward, she got another exciting phone call—Dick Jackson had agreed to meet with her. They spent a morning in his office discussing her manuscript for *Iggie's House*. He gave her suggestions for revising the book and offered to read it again when she had written a second draft. Inspired and driven, Blume went back to the typewriter, rewrote *Iggie's House* and sent it back to Jackson. He was pleased with her second draft and called to tell her he was going to publish the book. It was a day Blume describes as one that changed her life forever. She would forever feel grateful to Jackson and Wyndham, to whom she dedicated the book.

Indeed, that day in 1969 did change her life forever, kicking off a very long and successful writing career. Blume has written twenty-two books for children, middle graders, young adults, and adults that have collectively sold more than 70 million copies. She has won over ninety awards for her writing. Her first book, *The One in the Middle Is the Green Kangaroo*, has since been published in three different editions, each with different illustrations. Its initial success and the subsequent success it has garnered has far exceeded Blume's expectations for her own work.

But it would not be an exaggeration to say that Judy Blume is one of the most important authors of the twentieth century. Her works may not be considered "classic" literature, but reading them has become a rite of passage for children ever since the 1970s. Her impact on writing for young people is undeniable, but her impact on the very experience of growing up is deeply and personally felt. Years after reading a novel like *Deenie* or *Blubber*, an adult can still tell you why the book meant so much to him or her at the age of twelve. The reason? Blume always seemed to understand.

Blume's books explained why brothers and sisters fight, and why puberty can feel scary. Her work covers disabilities, alcoholism, divorce, bullying, premarital sex, eating disorders, and discrimination. Over the course of her writing career, she has tapped into situations that most readers can relate to—if not personally, then certainly through their friends and family. More than explaining right from wrong the way most children's authors did before her, her books describe the way life actually is.

Readers are drawn to characters who seem real, and Blume manages to get inside her characters' heads, writing just how it feels to be age nine, twelve, eighteen, or even forty-seven. Her books describe vivid people with unique predicaments. There's three-year-old Fudge swallowing a turtle in *Tales of a Fourth Grade Nothing*; ten-year-old Sheila confronting the horrors of a beginner's swimming test in *Otherwise Known as Sheila the Great*; and twelve-year-old Margaret stuffing her bra in *Are You There God? It's Me, Margaret*. To people who have grown up reading Judy Blume's books, these characters are as memorable and familiar as childhood friends.

People remember Judy Blume's books because they have a timeless quality. Since the 1970s when Blume first began to write, many things have changed, and some of the details in her books are no longer true in our lives today. For example, in *Freckle Juice*, Andrew gets ten cents for

Did you know...

Judy Blume's books have been translated into twenty-six different languages. *Iggie's House* has even been translated into Japanese.

his weekly allowance, a sum that now seems very small. In other books parents have to go to Nevada to get a divorce and mothers rarely work for a living. Today, divorce is legal in every state and many mothers work outside the home. But what hasn't changed is what it feels like to be a kid or a teenager, and in this way Blume's books remain fresh and realistic. Unlike the books of her childhood, Blume's books do not always tell happy and positive stories. Her characters have difficulties which they must learn to cope with.

Just as she hoped when she was sitting at her typewriter in those early days, Blume has written the kind of books that no one had written before her. And it has also been said that no children's book author who came after Judy Blume escaped her influence. Once she began to tell the truth about childhood and adolescence, other writers followed suit. Now that the taboos about children's literature had been broken, it would be difficult to return to the sort of books Judy Blume had read as a child.

Because they are so realistic, readers have responded strongly to Blume's books over the years. Seeing themselves on her books' pages, many young people have written her asking for advice. To children, Judy Blume can relate better than a teacher or parent. In fact, in 1986 Blume decided to compile an entire book of letters from her young fans. Titled *Letters to Judy*, the book was aimed at parents who wanted to know more about their kids' innermost feelings.

Today, over thirty years since those days of squeezing in writing between household chores and opening rejection letters, Judy Blume is famous throughout the world. It is easy now—after receiving heaps of awards, positive reviews, and international acclaim—to look back and remember with some fondness the people who doubted she had any talent. "I always say, be careful what you say to someone who wants to write, because you never know," she said.[4]

But after years of writing without knowing if anyone would ever truly be interested in her work, success is not something that Judy Blume takes for granted even today. She is still humbled by the devotion of her fans. "Every writer who connects with her readers is grateful. But I am especially grateful to have the most loyal and loving readers any writer could wish for," [5] she said.

Born in Elizabeth, New Jersey, in 1938, Blume grew up in the age of radio and movies—before the arrival of TV. She had always had a creative mind and envisioned herself as a performer. She even took dance lessons and tried to copy the moves of film star and swimmer Esther Williams (seen here).

2

Wallball,
New Jersey-Style

I didn't know anything about writers. It never occurred to me that they were regular people and that I could grow up to become one, even though I loved to make up stories inside my head. [6]
— *Judy Blume*

IT WAS LATE afternoon, and Judy Sussman had just gotten home from school. She was eight years old, a small skinny child whom many, including herself in later years, would describe as shy. Her friend Barry had walked her home the two blocks from school, as he always did to protect her from the dogs in the neighborhood, but he had to go home and do his schoolwork.

Her older brother would not be home for another hour. So she did what she always did when she had to play by herself. She took a small pink rubber ball and began bouncing it on the brick wall of her house. As she bounced the ball, she imagined a little girl just like her. She caught and bounced the ball over and over, and soon she had made up a story about this little girl becoming a famous dancer. The girl would travel the world and perform in *Swan Lake* to a standing ovation in between adventures in Paris and London.

It was the kind of story Judy made up often, but she never told to anyone else. Her stories were for her own benefit and she reserved them for times when she was alone. The stories made her feel less alone and less afraid. Storytelling was not limited to ball playing, though. She would make up stories while playing with paper dolls, creating fashion shows, and giving each character a name and history. When she was home sick from school, she would make up radio stories. Even when she was practicing piano she would pretend to give lessons to imaginary students, keeping a notebook on their progress with their scales and chords. Everything she did was an opportunity to use her imagination and dream up new characters. It was clear from a very early age that Judy Sussman had stories to tell.

Judy Blume was born Judy Sussman on February 12, 1938. Her parents, Rudolf and Esther Sussman, were a dentist and a homemaker, respectively. Judy had a brother named David who was four years older. David was a loner and more interested in working on science experiments in the basement than playing outside, and Judy found that she was the one who entertained her parents with her games and recitals, while her brother was considered the "smart one" in the family.

The Sussman family lived in Elizabeth, New Jersey, a

town just west of New York City. The Sussmans were Jewish, but though they celebrated most Jewish holidays they were not particularly religious. Judaism for the Sussmans was more about rituals than prayer. As she was growing up, Judy has said that she felt as though she was "always sitting shivah"—a reference to gathering to memorialize death in the Jewish tradition as a cousin, six aunts and uncles, and three grandparents died during her childhood. These were difficult times for her, and they added to her own sense of fear. With so many relatives dying, she was afraid that her parents would die, too.

A year after Judy was born, World War II began. Judy's father volunteered as an air-raid warden, an official in charge of notifying people of a war emergency, such as a bomb or a fire. The town would practice air raids in the middle of the night, and Judy would wake up to sirens. Judy's family would shut off all their lights and practice for the event of an actual enemy invasion. As a Jewish child, she grew to fear Adolph Hitler who had taken over Germany and was invading Europe while killing millions of Jews in concentration camps. For Jews living in America, like the Sussman family, it was a frightening time, and they felt help-less to stop the massacre overseas.

When Judy was seven, her family went on vacation and stayed at a boardinghouse in Bradley Beach, a resort town on the New Jersey shore. It was there that they heard the wonderful news that the war had ended. A celebration erupted into the streets, and there was a big party at the boardinghouse. But Judy did not feel like celebrating—

Did you know...

In 2000, Judy Blume wrote a foreword for a new edition of the Maud Hart Lovelace books, reminiscing about their importance during her childhood.

she was ill with a fever of 103 degrees. She missed the party outside while her mother put her to bed.

Though there were bleak times, there was plenty of fun in the Sussman household. Judy came home every day from school to have lunch with her mother. Over the summers she went to camp and made friends with other young girls from nearby towns. She loved to roller skate and watch baseball games. Every day she would listen to her favorite radio programs. These were the days before television, and the radio, with its plays and songs, sparked young Judy's imagination.

From an early age, Judy wanted to be a performer. "When I was growing up, I dreamed about becoming a cowgirl, a detective, a spy, a great actress, or a ballerina," she said. She took ballet and modern dance lessons, admired her movie star idols, particularly the swimming beauty Esther Williams and teen sensation Margaret O'Brien, and tried to copy their moves. She hoped that one day she would be able to perform onstage or on the big screen.

Her imagination was not limited to her show business aspirations, either. "I always had an active fantasy life, fueled by the movies. Following World War II, I fantasized about being a hero myself—a member of the Underground, fighting Hitler," [7] she said.

And then there were books. Judy's mother loved to read and spent every afternoon with a book. She was Judy's greatest influence in helping her gain an appreciation for books. Whenever she could, Judy would visit the public library and let herself get lost among the shelves. She enjoyed the Madeline books by Ludwig Bemelmans about the little French girl who becomes the hero of her orphanage. "I loved it so much, I didn't want to part with it," remembers Blume. "In fact, because I thought I had the only copy in the world, I hid the book in my kitchen toy drawer so that my mother wouldn't be able to return it to the library." [8] She also loved the Maud Hart Lovelace stories that described the adventures of Betsy, Tacy, and Tib. Every book demanded that she go on to the next one, and it was a habit she couldn't break. When she was a little older she read the Nancy Drew mysteries. Every week she would spend her allowance on books at the Ritz Bookstore in Elizabeth.

At first, books were a way to escape. Because she was so small, Judy felt out of place in school and often kept to herself. "Thin was not 'in' when I was growing up. The boys teased me, saying, 'If Judy swallowed an olive, she'd look pregnant.'" [9] She was timid and afraid of dogs, thunderstorms, and the dark. Books, like her wallball games, were something she could do on her own, and they felt safe. It wasn't until she started fourth grade that Judy began to open up and become less shy.

Though she shared her mother's love of reading, Judy was closer to her father. Her father, who she called Doey-bird, was lively and saw life as an adventure. Her mother, on the other hand, was quiet and usually worried. Judy at times felt she was overprotective, while her father encouraged her to live fully and experience as much as possible. Perhaps because she admired him so much, Judy would grow up to be more like her father.

When Judy was about nine years old, her brother David became sick with a kidney infection and the doctor suggested the family move to a warmer climate to help him get better. Judy, her mother, grandmother, and brother prepared to move to Miami Beach, Florida. Her father would stay behind in New Jersey to work, visiting the family in Florida once a month.

This was a particularly difficult change for Judy. While she looked forward to the tropical weather of Florida and the adventure ahead, she was worried. At this time her father was forty-two years old and both of his brothers had died at that very age. Being apart from him meant that she would not be there to make sure he was healthy. So Judy did what she could to ensure his safety from a distance: She prayed seven times every day that her father would not die.

The family found a pink stucco apartment building that had a goldfish pond in the courtyard. Judy and her brother shared the living room, sleeping on daybeds. Judy had never seen palm trees before and she grew to love the beach that was so much warmer and softer than the beaches of the Jersey shore. In Miami, Judy would play outside every day until it grew dark. She would rollerskate to the music broadcast in Flamingo Park and go to the beach on weekends. Even though she missed her father terribly, the two years spent in Miami were an exciting time for her, and she would always remember it fondly. In the end, it turned out her fears about her father would not come to pass—he turned forty-three that year and escaped the family curse.

As she got older, Judy began to notice that there were certain secrets that adults concealed. One day Judy saw her mother reading a book called *A Rage to Live* by John O'Hara. She asked her mother about the book and she was told never to read it until she became an adult. As her mother had always encouraged her to read in the past, Judy was surprised at her reaction and wondered what could be in the book that made it off-limits.

There were other times when she felt that adults were withholding the truth from her. One day, when she was nine, her parents went to visit an aunt and uncle on Long Island. When they got there, Judy's cousin Grace, who was thirteen years old, complained that she wasn't feeling well. When Judy asked what was wrong, Grace told her only that she would find out when she was thirteen. "On the long drive

Although Blume's parents had always encouraged her to read, she soon learned that some books were off-limits to young readers. A Rage to Live *by John O'Hara (seen here) was one such book. Blume saw that there were few books that spoke frankly to young readers — a problem she sought to correct in her own writing.*

back to New Jersey I asked my parents over and over again *what* I would find out when I was thirteen. They kept changing the subject." [10] Finally, her father sat down and tried to explain menstruation to her, but Judy did not understand.

When Judy was in sixth grade she began to be curious about her body and some of the changes she and her friends were going through. She looked up the word "sex" in the encyclopedia. All she could find were drawings of plants that showed how they performed their process of reproduction. Judy's mother never discussed sex or puberty or menstruation. Judy's father tried to be open with her, but he never explained what she really wanted to know.

Judy began to talk to her friends. They too were having similar feelings and fears about their bodies. The more she talked to them at camp and at school, she realized that they were all going through the same thing and they were all looking for more answers. Eventually, her friend Roxie's mother gave her a book about menstruation, which Judy and Roxie would look through together. It didn't answer all their questions, but they were grateful to have it. Judy wondered what all the fuss was about and why it was so difficult to learn the truth. To Judy, that particular year—with all its confusion and questions—was the most important year of her life, and she would remember it vividly for decades afterward.

When Judy got older she was still creative, although she describes this era as less exciting. As a teenager, she became more interested in fitting in—wearing nice clothes and meeting boys—than in making up stories. But she was active in school. She was the coeditor of the school's newspaper, sang in chorus, danced in the school dance troupe, and performed in school plays.

During her junior year in high school, she got a reading list from her English teacher and found that John O'Hara's name was on it. Remembering the incident with her mother she rushed to the Elizabeth Public Library to find *A Rage to Live*. The librarian told her that it was kept in a locked closet, and if she wanted to take it out she needed a written permission slip from her mother. Judy was sure her mother would not consent to signing a permission slip, and she was angry and confused that the library, a place where students were supposed to read, would keep a book from her.

When she graduated from high school, Judy was accepted to Boston University. The idea, according to her mother and most young women at the time, was to go to college to meet a husband. If that didn't work out, she would get a teaching degree in the meantime to fall back on. Teaching was then considered a proper career for women, at a time when women did not typically have careers outside the home.

But her time at Boston University was short-lived. She was there for only two weeks when she fell ill with mononucleosis and had to return to New Jersey. The next year she transferred to New York University. In the meantime, her parents moved from her childhood home in Elizabeth to another house in Westfield, New Jersey. On a visit home from college to the new house during her junior year, Judy met John Blume, a young attorney. He was her first love, and they dated for a few months before planning their wedding for the summer before her senior year.

In July, the family went to pick up David and his then-pregnant wife at the airport. When they got home, Judy's father went to lie down, saying he didn't feel well. He then suddenly died of a heart attack—at age fifty-four. Judy, who had been close to her father, was heartbroken.

Judy and John went on with the wedding plans, noting that her father would have wanted them to celebrate, and the Blumes were married in a small ceremony in her parents' house. She had come a long way from her days as a skinny child throwing a ball against her house. She was no longer shy, and she was now a wife. Still, Judy Blume missed her childhood and longed for the days when her imagination took over. It would not be long, though, before she figured out a way to recapture it.

By the late 1960s, the feminist movement in America was gaining strength, and protests like the one shown here were commonplace. Blume—a housewife and mother in suburban New Jersey—was going through her own rebellion of sorts. Deeply in need of a creative outlet, she turned to writing, drawing on her own childhood experiences to create her second novel, Are You There God? It's Me, Margaret.

3

Margaret and Sally

I'd published two books and several short stories before Margaret, *but I hadn't found my voice yet. I hadn't written from deep inside. With* Margaret *I found my voice and my audience.* [11]
—*Judy Blume*

BY THE TIME she graduated from college, Blume was pregnant with her first child. Motherhood and life as a homemaker had enveloped her before she even realized what was happening. Judy and John moved to a garden apartment in Plainfield, New Jersey, which was close to his law office. Their daughter, Randy, was born in 1961. Two years later the family of three moved to a house in Scotch Plains just a few miles away. There, Blume gave birth to their second child—their son, Larry.

As a housewife in suburban New Jersey, Blume felt bored. She was not interested in playing golf or tennis as the other young wives and mothers around her did. Nor was she interested in going shopping, which was the other favorite activity for the women in her neighborhood. Like Blume, many of these women had been taught to grow up to get married instead of being encouraged to pursue study and careers.

But now in the late 1960s, women were beginning to question their role as stay-at-home moms. In Blume's life, this was happening on a small, individual scale. She did not realize that a feminist movement was in its beginning stages—much of it happening just across the river in New York City. She only knew that she was unhappy. While the other housewives seemed as dissatisfied as she was, no one she knew complained about their situation. "I don't think any of us at that time ever admitted what we were feeling or what life was like or what our hopes and dreams were," [12] she said.

Blume was determined to make her life more interesting. She tried for a time to write songs. When that didn't work out, she started making banners for children by gluing squares of felt together. She sold several of these to Bloomingdale's, but she did not feel satisfied by this work. She eventually got an allergic rash from the glue, so she began thinking up children's stories and illustrating them with colored pencils.

Then the flier arrived, advertising the children's writing class at NYU, and before long, Blume had taken the class twice and written and published two books. Still, she didn't feel confident about her skills and wondered how long it would take before she believed that she was really and truly a writer. Somehow it still felt like a game she was playing. Neither book had exploded in popularity, and her self-doubt from years of rejection and comments from naysayers left her feeling insecure about her new career. Had she just been lucky with her first two books? What if no one wanted to publish her work again, or worse, what if she couldn't come up with any more good ideas?

By 1970—even before *Iggie's House* was published— Blume had decided that her next book would be about sixth grade, which to her was still the most vivid year of her life. She thought about all her insecurities involving puberty and boys, and her worries and fears in the year that she was twelve. As she sat down to write, a novel poured out of her almost as if by magic. She began with her notebook sketch-ings and observations, and moved on to the typewriter. All the feelings and thoughts came rushing back, and before she knew it, she had completed another novel.

The result was *Are You There God? It's Me, Margaret*. For the first time, Blume was thrilled with the book and felt confident about her own work. Says Blume of the book, "*Margaret* was the first book I wrote where I said 'O.K., now I write from my own experience,' and that's when I started to grow, as a writer and as a woman." [13] She gave the manuscript to Dick Jackson, the editor who had helped her publish *Iggie's House*. She didn't yet have a title for the book, but the typist in Jackson's office filled in the title space with the book's first line and it stuck.

Are You There God? It's Me, Margaret is the story of an almost twelve-year-old girl whose family moves from New York City to suburban New Jersey. Margaret makes new friends who induct her into the PTS (Pre-Teen Sensation) club where the girls discuss menstruation, bras, and boys. As the new girl, Margaret is anxious about fitting in with the

PTS club. She knows somehow that she is a little different from the other girls. For one thing, she is half-Jewish and half-Christian, while all the other girls go to church and Sunday school. Margaret's parents don't celebrate any religious holidays, and they don't want her to be religious at all. Margaret is curious about religion and even goes into New York with her grandmother to visit a synagogue. She doesn't know which god she prays to but she talks to God anyway, confiding her worries and fears about growing up, and life in her new town.

The character of Margaret Simon was different in many ways from Blume herself, who grew up with two Jewish parents and had a brother, but her anxiety about her body and her conversations with God were straight out of Judy's own childhood. "That is something I did as a kid, talk to God. She [Margaret] is concerned with her body, wants her period, wants to have her breasts develop. All of that was on my mind when I was twelve," she told interviewer Don Swaim.

Judy Blume's first book, *The One in the Middle Is the Green Kangaroo*, was a picture book intended for young children. With *Margaret*, Blume was targeting preteens as she had with *Iggie's House*, presenting serious subjects to children between the ages of ten and twelve in a manner that they could understand.

While *Iggie's House* dealt with racism and discrimination, *Margaret* tackled menstruation and puberty. At the time when it was published, no books had tried to speak about these topics in a positive and realistic way. Only one book for young readers, *The Long Secret* by Louise Fitzhugh—a writer Judy Blume admired—had discussed menstruation. The passage in Fitzhugh's book, published five years before *Margaret*, was more focused on explaining the biological facts to its readers than the feelings of girls who have already begun or are anticipating menstruation. If anything, it made the idea of menstruation sound scarier and more threatening.

In *Margaret*, the emphasis is on the emotions stirred up by the physical changes of adolescence. Margaret begs God to speed the arrival of her period and help her breasts grow, praying "Are you there God? It's me, Margaret. I just told my mother I want a bra. Please help me grow God. You know where. I want to be like everyone else." [*Are You There*, p. 37] To Margaret, her period is not so much scary as it is a mysterious symbol that she is convinced will improve her life. When she gets her period it will be a sign that she is normal and like all the other girls at school.

When she was writing *Margaret*, Blume did not consider menstruation a controversial or even a surprising topic for a book for young adults. She was simply writing about her own experience as a twelve-year-old and conjuring up the book she would have wanted to read then.

When it was published, *Are You There God? It's Me, Margaret* was met with both criticism and admiration. Reviewers admired the natural dialogue and the realistic description of the feelings of adolescence. Others complained that Margaret was too self-centered and that her calls to God were offensive. And there were those who felt the discussion of menstruation and puberty was a topic that was too mature for children. Still, at the end of 1970, it was named an Outstanding Book of the Year by the *New York Times*. When it was

Did you know...

Besides being chosen as a *New York Times* Outstanding Book of the Year (1970), *Are You There God? It's Me, Margaret* has won the Nene Award (1975), the Young Hoosier Book Award (1976), and the North Dakota Children's Choice Award (1979).

published in paperback two years later, *Margaret* exploded in popularity. That was the moment the cult of Judy Blume began and her readership increased exponentially.

Finally, Blume felt like a real writer. People were taking her work seriously whether they loved it or hated it. In 1971, she received her first fan letter from a thirteen-year-old girl who wrote that Margaret Simon was the first character in any book that she could identify with. Soon, a flood of letters from her young readers began pooling in her mailbox. Blume had written something her readers understood and they responded.

Seven years and seven books later, Judy Blume would again use her own experiences as the basis for another heroine—ten-year-old Sally J. Freedman. In *Starring Sally J. Freedman as Herself*, the title character is a young girl in 1947 who spends her winter in Miami. The family moves to help Sally's brother Douglas recuperate from a kidney infection, and they leave Sally's father, a dentist, behind in New Jersey. The first scene is taken from Judy's stay in Bradley Beach, when World War II ended, and Sally gets sick while her neighbors are celebrating.

With Sally, Judy Blume relived her years in Florida. Douglas was modeled after Judy's brother David. Like David, Douglas is a loner who spends his time in a basement workshop—so much time that he gets a sunburn on the back of his neck from the workbench lamp. The grandmother in the book is also modeled after Judy Blume's grandmother. She speaks Yiddish, saying phrases that Judy Blume's grandmother used to say. Sally's mother is cautious and worrisome, while her father is adventurous and fun-loving. Sally—as Judy did at her age—adores Esther Williams, dances, and rollerskates. She organizes a dance program for charity with both her mother and grandmother contributing.

Sally's father is forty-two years old, and she worries that he will die as his brothers did at the same age, so she routinely prays that he will not die while her family is separated. This idea, too, came straight out of Judy Blume's own childhood.

"I have this capacity for total recall," she told Sybil Steinberg of *Publishers Weekly*. "That's my talent, if there's a talent involved. I have this gift, this memory, so it's easy to project myself back to certain stages of my life. And I write about what I know is true of kids going through those same stages."

A major theme in *Starring Sally J. Freedman as Herself* is a fear of war. As a Jewish child, Sally is well aware that Hitler and his Third Reich killed millions of Jews in World War II, and she has grown up afraid of Hitler. In the book, the war has ended, but when Sally meets her neighbor, Mr. Zavodsky, she imagines that he is actually Hitler in disguise and is hiding out from the Allies in Miami Beach.

While this was not something that happened to Judy Blume, the fantasy is very much in keeping with the kind of child she was at Sally's age. Blume, in fact, has said that the book explains how and why she became a writer. Like Blume at her age, Sally is imaginative and likes to make up stories.

Starring Sally J. Freedman as Herself did not receive good reviews. Critics found Sally's obsession with Hitler morbid and felt that Blume's descriptions of her fantasies were too violent. Others read it as being too autobiographical and not interesting enough to young readers at that time—they felt that children would not be able to relate to a girl in the 1940s. Readers, on the other hand, seemed to like Sally and her vivid imagination, though the response to the book was not as strong as it had been for *Are You There God? It's Me, Margaret.*

For her book Starring Sally J. Freedman as Herself, *Blume returned to her childhood experiences during World War II. The character of Sally reflected the fears experienced by Jews in the shadow of Adolph Hitler (seen here). In the book, the war has ended, but Sally imagines that her neighbor is actually Hitler in disguise, hiding from the Allies in Miami Beach, Florida.*

"The children who love Sally are like Sally. I get two kinds of letters about *Sally*—either 'Sally is such a weird kid' or 'I'm just like Sally.' When you are that kind of child you're very careful not to let other people know," [14] said Blume.

Margaret and Sally were Judy Blume's two most autobiographical characters. To readers they were a comfort: honest, open young girls with familiar problems. In another way, Margaret and Sally are role models. In both books, adults are often secretive and confusing, trying to protect children from the truth they are already aware of, but Margaret and Sally are refreshingly forthcoming. Just as their creator did at her age, they keep asking questions until they find out what they need to know.

In between *Are You There God? It's Me, Margaret* and *Starring Sally J. Freedman as Herself*, Judy Blume wrote many different kinds of books for different kinds of readers, but to the preteen crowd, these two would remain memorable for years afterward. For Judy Blume, her two autobiographical heroines would be among her most favorite characters.

Judy, remarking on *Margaret*'s surprising longevity, would later tell Carolyn Mackler and *Ms.* magazine, "When I wrote *Margaret*, it never dawned on me that twenty-eight years later kids would still be reading it. But it's about feelings and anticipating growing up, and those things never change."

JUDY BLUME

Freckle Juice

The title for Blume's book Freckle Juice *came from her daughter Randy. A lighthearted book,* Freckle Juice *was a departure from the difficult situations often faced by Blume's other characters.*

4

Stories From the Tub

Everybody thinks they're normal. You pretend, like everybody else, I'm normal. But inside you know you're not, the harder you try to be. And you're afraid to be yourself because there is no yourself. You don't even know who yourself is. [15]

—Judy Blume

IN 1971, JUDY Blume—now energized and encouraged by the success of *Are You There God? It's Me, Margaret*—began writing at a furious pace, churning out at least one book a year. She had fans now, and they were waiting eagerly for her every word. *Margaret* was followed by the equally contemplative *Then*

43

Again, Maybe I Won't, which drew from similar themes but dealt with them from a boy's point of view. Blume felt that with *Margaret* she had "found her voice," which was in fact the voice of real adolescents and their problems. This time, she wanted to explore the experience of boys at the same age.

In *Then Again,* Tony Miglione is a working-class thirteen-year-old living in Jersey City, New Jersey. His electrician father stumbles on an invention that brings sudden wealth to Tony's family. They move to an affluent suburb where Tony must adapt to a very different lifestyle. His family, in an attempt to fit in, makes their own changes. His father gets rid of his electrician's truck when a neighbor asks if they are "getting work done" at their house, and his mother, whose name is Carmella, allows the neighbors to call her Carol. Tony suspects that they are hypocritical in turning their back on their past as a less wealthy family, but he has other problems to confront. As in *Margaret,* Tony must navigate the territory of a new school and new friends, all the while trying to adapt to the bodily changes of puberty, including uncontrollable erections and wet dreams. Even worse is that his new friend in town shoplifts, and Tony does not know what to make of it.

With *Then Again,* Blume was writing about the loneliness and frustration kids feel when they are not in control of their own lives. She has said that it was a difficult book for her to write because of its multiple themes and issues, and perhaps also because it was her first attempt at capturing a boy's point of view. *Then Again* received much the same response as its predecessor. Readers, especially boys, were eager to find a book that was true to their experiences. Critics again objected to Blume's frankness about puberty and complained that she was becoming predictable.

As if to avoid falling into such a formula, Judy Blume then turned her attention back to writing for younger children.

While writing for a younger audience dictated that her subject matter was more upbeat, she still refused to pretend that children led perfect and carefree lives. If Judy Blume had a mission, it was to continue to tell the truth about childhood. These books, though humorous, remained focused on the reality of being a kid.

During this time, Blume wrote *Freckle Juice,* the story of a second grader named Andrew who envies his friend Nicky's freckles. When he asks Nicky how he got them, another classmate sells him a recipe for freckle juice for fifty cents, claiming the magic elixir will bring on the spots. The recipe of course does not work, and Andrew must find another way to create freckles.

The idea for the book came from Blume's own home. "I had a great title, thanks to my daughter Randy, who used to play in the bathtub making a mess with shampoo, soap, and powder," recalled Blume. "She called this concoction freckle juice." [16] Once she had the title, it was only a short while before she conjured up the story to go with it. The end product was a lively and lighthearted book, illustrated with pictures of the ever-hopeful Andrew.

Blume would write another comic story the following year, the idea for which also came from her home. This one was in the form of a short novel for elementary school readers called *Tales of a Fourth Grade Nothing.* Blume recalled:

When I began to write, our babysitter, Willie Mae Bartlett, brought me an article from the newspaper about a toddler who swallowed a tiny pet turtle. This was in the late '60s, when you could still buy turtles for pets. Willie Mae thought the story might inspire me. And it certainly did! I sat down and wrote a picture book called "Peter, Fudge and Dribble." I submitted my manuscript to several publishers but they all rejected it. Two editors wrote personal notes saying they found the story very funny but one was concerned that it could lead to small children swallowing turtles, and the other found it too unbelievable to publish.

A few years later, my first agent submitted the story to Ann Durell, editor of children's books at E.P. Dutton. Ann invited me to lunch. I was so nervous I could hardly eat but she was so warm and friendly I finally relaxed. Ann liked my story but she suggested, instead of a picture book, I consider writing a longer book about the Hatcher family, using "Peter, Fudge and Dribble" as one of the chapters.[17]

Blume spent that summer writing the book. The story was about a fourth grader named Peter Hatcher who feels upstaged by his younger brother Fudge. Fudge is the turtle-swallower in the family and always seems to get everyone's attention with his outrageous antics. Peter, on the other hand, feels ignored and left out.

"My biggest problem is my brother Farley Drexel Hatcher," says Peter Hatcher in *Tales*, " . . . Fudge is always in my way. He messes up everything he sees. And when he gets mad he throws himself flat on the floor and he screams. *And* he kicks. *And* he bangs his fists. The only time I really like him is when he's sleeping. He sucks four fingers on his left hand and makes a slurping noise." [*Tales of a Fourth Grade Nothing*, p. 4]

Tales is set in Manhattan, and Blume housed her fictional family in the building where her best friend, Mary Weaver, lived. The character of Fudge—comical to readers, but infinitely irritating to Peter—was based on Blume's son, Larry, when he was a toddler.

The book proved immensely appealing to its third- and fourth-grade readers. With her earlier work, Judy Blume had shown her ability to handle sensitive topics, but now she showed that she had a great sense of humor that children enjoyed. They could relate to Peter, who, like most children, quibbles with his siblings and would like to be the object of attention. Many readers were equally intrigued by Sheila Tubman, a neighbor girl who is Peter Hatcher's enemy. Blume did not expect Sheila to be so popular with readers, and said, "I was surprised when I started getting letters about Sheila. After all, she has a fairly small part in *Tales*. But kids wanted to know more about her." [18]

Blume responded to her fans' pleas in 1972 with *Otherwise Known as Sheila the Great*. Sheila is yet another young Blume character who is troubled by worries and fears. Sheila is afraid of dogs and swimming, and she must face both during her family's summer vacation in a rented house in upstate New York. When she's around other people, Sheila covers up her fear with bravado and brags that she is not afraid of anything. While the book is entertaining and comical in the same manner as *Tales of a Fourth Grade Nothing*, it addresses some of the insecurities children feel about being afraid and letting others know.

Up to this point in her writing career, Blume had been relying on her memory to create characters like Margaret and Tony, but more and more she was looking to her children for ideas. As they were getting older and expressing themselves in more direct ways, she realized that much of her subject matter was available right at home. She noticed her children were dealing with some of the same experiences she remembered from childhood: wanting to fit in while trying to find their own identity, craving attention but not wanting to stand out, and feeling the sense of power from growing up but feeling powerless around adults. Like most of her characters, they wanted to be normal but found that it was not always that easy.

Sometimes, she found, kids' problems were the direct result of their parents' problems. In the early 1970s, divorce rates were skyrocketing as Americans began to question the idea of marriage for the first time. Women inspired by the feminist movement were going to work outside the home, and both men and women began to admit their dissatisfaction with the relationships they had rushed into right out of high school or college; expecting to get married as young as their parents had. But it was now more socially acceptable to admit that a marriage was not working.

All around Blume's neighborhood, couples were breaking up. Many of the women who were staying home and going shopping just a few years earlier were now faced with the dilemmas of custody and single parenting. Blume's own children witnessed their friends' parents splitting up and began to come home with questions for their parents. They wanted to know why this was happening and if their own parents were going to break up.

"I tried to reassure them, but I wasn't really sure myself. I wrote *It's Not the End of the World* at that time, to try to answer some of my children's questions about divorce, to let other kids know that they were not alone, and, perhaps, because I was not happy in my marriage," Blume wrote in *Letters to Judy*.

It's Not the End of the World, published in 1972, is the story of Karen Newman, a sixth grader whose parents are always fighting. Soon she learns that they are going to get a separation, and she and her siblings must learn to cope with the possibility of their getting a divorce. The title comes from the book's last sentence, in which Karen decides that while her parents splitting up is difficult and painful, it might be the best thing for everyone involved.

The book was written as much for her children as it was

for herself, and it allowed Blume to explore the topic before she had really come to terms with its significance in her own life. "At the time," said Blume, "my own marriage was in trouble, but I wasn't ready or able to admit it to myself, let alone anyone else. In the hope that it would get better, I dedicated this book to my husband." [19]

Blume had broken new ground again. Because it was largely a contemporary phenomenon and because it was complicated subject matter, no children's author before had written about divorce and its effect on children. Readers were grateful that she broke the silence. Letters came pouring in, thanking her for making divorce seem a little less scary.

Yet another young adult book, *Deenie*, followed. *Deenie* is the story of an attractive young girl who plans on becoming a model. Deenie is a normal, attractive teenager but finds out that she has scoliosis and must wear a brace. While Deenie is upset about the development, her mother, who has been calling her the "beautiful one" (and her sister the "smart one") her whole life is even more devastated than Deenie. Blume had met a family in a similar situation and was struck by the mother's response. More than a book about scoliosis, *Deenie* is about the difficulty of living up to parental pressures and expectations.

Deenie also contained the following passage where Deenie takes a bath and touches herself: "Usually I take showers and get in and out as fast as possible. But the hot water was very relaxing and soon I began to enjoy it. I reached

> **Did you know...**
>
> The original title for *Tales of a Fourth Grade Nothing* was *Peter, Fudge and Dribble*. Judy Blume and her editor decided to change it when another book called *Peter Potts* came out that year.

down and touched my special place with the washcloth. I rubbed and rubbed until I got that good feeling." [*Deenie*, p. 132] Parents and teachers were very upset that Blume had described a girl masturbating even though many books before *Deenie* had discussed male masturbation in terms more frank than "special place." Blume defended the scene to her critics saying that it came straight out of her own experience, and that she considered masturbation for girls not only completely natural, but a valid experience to write about for teens who might be worried that it wasn't.

Three years after Blume's daughter Randy invented freckle juice, she would provide the inspiration for a different kind of story. As Blume tells it, Randy was a quiet and sensitive ten-year-old. But some troubling things were happening in her fifth-grade class, and Randy would come home from school with daily reports about her fellow students. Blume recalled, "Randy was especially upset by the way one girl in her class, Cindy, had become the victim of the class leader. One day during lunch period the leader of the class and her group locked Cindy in a supply closet and held a mock trial." [20]

Blume was shocked by her daughter's story, particularly by the teacher's inability to quell the situation, and she decided her next book would be about bullying in the classroom. The result was the novel *Blubber*, in which a group of students taunt another student, Linda, for being overweight. Blume wrote a scene into the book where Linda is locked into the closet and put on trial. The book is told through the perspective of Jill, who, like Randy, witnesses the events around her but feels powerless to stop them. Jill actually takes part in the teasing until she herself becomes a target for the bully.

Decades before school shootings would provoke national discussion about bullying, Blume had dealt with the subject unflinchingly. She had also resisted making a strong and obvious judgment in the book, instead allowing her readers to come to their own conclusions about bullying. But when *Blubber* was released, critics took aim at Blume for not setting a "moral tone." They claimed that her matter-of-fact description of the students' mean behavior could be used as a manual for bullies.

Other people saw the value in a book that described what can happen in a school situation without telling kids how to feel. They felt that it was precisely because Blume did not lecture her readers that they would react positively to the book. *Blubber* has since been used in some teaching programs to prepare young teachers for some of the dynamics of the classroom. Other teachers have had their students read the book in order to initiate a discussion about bullying. Said Blume, "When I began this book I was determined to write the truth about the school-bus culture in the language of that culture. *Blubber* is funny to a point, then wham! Some adults are bothered by the language and the cruelty, but the kids get it. They live it." [21]

Within the span of a few short years, Judy Blume had become a highly regarded and prolific author for children of different age groups. Her success had not come without its share of risk-taking and criticism. With every risk she took and every new topic she broached people were meeting her with skepticism. But her early days of resisting negative voices had stuck with her, and she was determined not to let what people said affect her work. Despite her successes, she refused to sit back and stick with a formula, and instead wrote very different kinds of books, each with their own set of difficulties. She was widening her scope as a writer and reaching out to more children every day.

Many books about teenage sexuality had been, until the 1970s, cautionary tales that ended in tragedy. When her daughter Randy asked Blume to take a more honest look at relationships, she responded with Forever, *which examined the issues of sexuality, including birth control. Despite being criticized for its frankness, the book was an instant success. Shown here are Stephanie Zimbalist and Dean Butler who starred in the 1978 made-for-television adaptation of* Forever.

5

Tough Topics

I hate to categorize books . . . I wish that older readers would read my books about young people, and I hope that younger readers will grow up to read what I have to say about adult life. I'd like to feel that I write for everybody. [22]

—*Judy Blume*

IN THE MID-1970S, Blume's now teenage children continued to inspire her writing. At the age of fourteen, Blume's daughter Randy came across a number of books about premarital sex that all had the same theme: a young girl decided to lose her virginity—not because she was in love, but because it was a way to rebel. These stories, most of which had been written in the late 1960s as a response to growing numbers of teenage pregnancies, always seemed to end with the girl getting heartbroken or pregnant or both. But in the 1970s these books seemed ridiculously naïve as well as outdated.

Randy was sure that these books, which conveyed only the most negative attitudes toward premarital sex, did not tell the whole story. She was curious about sexuality, just like her mother had been at her age, and she wanted adults to tell her the truth instead of trying to scare her or hide the facts. Randy approached her mother and asked if she could write a more realistic story about sex. Recalls Blume, "She said, 'Couldn't there ever be a book about two nice, smart kids who do it, and nobody has to die?' I thought, yeah, we're not doing anybody any favor by all of this sex linked with punishment." [23]

Judy Blume had dealt with racism, scoliosis, bullying, puberty, and divorce. But now she would tackle a topic that was foremost on teenagers' minds. The feminist movement and the sexual revolution in the 1970s had made discussion of sex more open than it ever had been before, but teenagers were still in many cases being protected from the most important information. The result was a rising number of teen pregnancies and a number of teenagers who were sexually active but not informed about what they were doing. Blume felt that the lack of information and education was what caused the kind of unhappy endings described in her daughter's books. At her daughter's urging, Blume decided to write a book about premarital sex in which the couple gives the decision careful consideration. The couple would discuss birth control. The girl would not be punished for her decision to have intercourse with her boyfriend.

The book, *Forever*, told the story of a young couple, Michael and Katharine, who meet at a party. Their relationship grows into a warm, tenderhearted affair and after several months of dating, they decide to lose their virginity with one another. The experience is a positive one. Katharine discusses it with her mother and decides to go to a doctor beforehand for birth control pills. Eventually, though, Katharine goes away to summer camp where she meets another man. When she returns home, she breaks up with Michael. In Judy Blume's story of young romance and sex, the boy is the one who ends up heartbroken.

The instant popularity of *Forever* surprised Judy Blume. Even though she had recognized a need for the story, she was not altogether thrilled with the final result. As the only book she was "asked" to write, *Forever* felt less personal to her than some of her other works. Readers, however, did not see it that way, and word spread that here was a book that finally handled premarital sex realistically. *Forever* flew off the shelves.

In 1975, at the time when *Forever* was published, there wasn't a "Young Adult" category of literature. Blume wrote the book with thirteen- and fourteen-year-old readers in mind, but her publisher labeled it "Judy Blume's first novel for adults" on its jacket. In many bookstores, *Forever* was mistakenly displayed next to her other books, all of which had targeted a much younger audience. It wasn't long before complaints began rolling in. Librarians, parents, and teachers started to complain about the mature content of Blume's latest book. Comparing her to a 1970s author of pulpy, soap opera-like books, her detractors dubbed Blume the "Jacqueline Susann of children's books." Some of them accused Blume of using sex to sell her book while others accused her of encouraging teens to have premarital sex.

Blume felt the opposite was true—that by presenting the facts about sex she was allowing teens to make informed decisions. In an interview with *Boldtype*, she said, "I guess it's better to have your first sexual experience between the covers of a book, then between the covers of a bed. It's better to read about it first, then do it. I think a lot of people read about sex and satisfy their curiosity, so when the time comes, they know to be more responsible. They understand what's happening." [24]

At the same time, Blume was concerned that others would see the success of *Forever* and try to use sex as a way to sell books. To her, *Forever* was not so much about sex as it was about the relationship between young people and the decisions they must make. In interviews, she has continued to encourage teenagers to wait until they finish high school to have sex.

In recent times, Blume has also been concerned that *Forever* is not an accurate model for today's readers. Reflecting the era when it was written, the biggest concern for Katharine and Michael was pregnancy. Today, however, Blume notes that times have changed and teenagers need to be concerned about sexually transmitted diseases, including HIV. Katharine's birth control pills are no longer sufficient protection.

Still, *Forever* has been used in school sex education programs—not as a manual for birth control but as a way of explaining the feelings attached to sex. Blume has also received many letters from parents thanking her for writing a book that can be used to help them discuss sex with their children. Yet again her writing had filled a need, addressing problems that had, before her, been absent in young people's literature.

In the meantime, Blume had to face some of her own problems. While her professional life was better than ever, her personal life was coming to a crisis point. Despite her efforts to assure her children and herself that everything was all right, Blume finally admitted that her sixteen-year marriage was over. In 1975, Judy and John Blume decided to get a divorce.

Blume was deeply depressed and anxious about starting her life over on her own. At first she stayed in New Jersey and her children visited her husband on the weekends. But six months after her divorce, Judy Blume met a scientist named Thomas Kitchens. Blume saw this as an opportunity to escape her life in the suburbs and make a fresh start. She married him right away and moved with her children to England for six months, where Kitchens had found some temporary work at a university. It was the first time she had done—and not just written about—something truly daring. As she told Don Swaim, "I ran away to see the world. At thirty-seven I did what I should have done at seventeen or twenty-two."

From England, Judy, Thomas, and her children moved to Santa Fe, New Mexico, where Kitchens had gotten a new job. Blume tried to convince her children that this was the beginning of a wonderful new life for them, but inside she was not convinced. Already, the relationship between Blume and Kitchens had grown rocky, and they fought often. She soon came to realize that she had rushed into the marriage without really getting to know him. She had remarried out of fear of being alone and a desire to start over. For the next few years, as she contemplated her choices, Judy Blume slowed down her writing output. She put out only one book during this time, *Starring Sally J. Freedman as Herself.*

> ### Did you know...
>
> After fielding many offers, Blume sold the film rights to *Forever* in 1978. The book was turned into a made-for-television movie which was filmed in San Francisco and starred a young actress named Stephanie Zimbalist as Katharine.

Then, in 1978, Judy Blume did something very different. She wrote a novel called *Wifey*, which described her experience not as a child or teenager, but as an adult. She called this book her first work for adult readers—the story of her own rebellion. In *Wifey*, Sandy Pressman is a suburban housewife who is bored and dissatisfied with her marriage and her life. Like Judy Blume in her early years of marriage, she is expected to play golf and tennis, but she is a failure at both. Unable to admit that the perfect life she expected is beyond her grasp, Sandy begins to act out her frustrations. First, she imagines that she has a series of different exotic illnesses and then she has some unsuccessful extramarital affairs.

Wifey is in many ways a comical book that exaggerates the confined feeling of a woman stuck in an unhappy marriage. Sandy's husband demands that she serve him certain dinners according to the days of week and that she keep a chart of their dog's bowel movements. But despite its humorous tone, Blume's reasons for writing the book were deeply serious. She wanted to get at the truth of unhappy marriage. While she had managed to leave her own marriage, she recognized that many women did not see divorce as an option. Blume explained this to Linda Bird Francke in a *Newsweek* interview, saying, "There are three women I called when my first husband and I were splitting up, and they all cried. 'Oh God, you're so lucky,' they said. 'You have a way of getting out.' So this book is for them. They just continue to live lives of quiet desperation, and at least saying it, getting it out in the open, is a step."

As with *Forever,* there was some concern that young readers would want to read *Wifey* simply because its author was a familiar and popular name to children. The same year, in fact, six of Blume's paperbacks were on juvenile best-seller lists. People who were concerned that children would be exposed to *Wifey*'s adult themes have asked Judy Blume why she did not have the book published under a pseudonym. She has responded that she felt it was important to be honest about this other, more grown-up side of her experience.

Blume knew that *Wifey* was a career risk. She was testing out a whole new audience and revealing extremely personal feelings in the process. "When *Wifey* was published some people thought I would never write another children's book, some thought I had written a real book at last, some were angry that I hadn't used a pseudonym, others that I even had such thoughts! Plus, I began to hear from old boyfriends."[25]

As it turned out, *Wifey* was a risk worth taking. Critics loved the book and noted their surprise that Blume could write so convincingly for adults. In many ways, though, *Wifey* fit right in with the rest of Judy Blume's work. Adults were responding to the same quality so many children before them had loved about Blume's writing—her honesty. Blume herself explained the phenomenon neatly to *Publishers Weekly*. "I think that my appeal has to do with feelings and with character identification. Things like that don't change from generation to generation. That's what I really know."

The success of *Wifey* was energizing. Still, Blume's professional success could not compensate for her increasingly unfulfilling personal life. She felt that her second marriage had been a terrible mistake, but for three-and-a-half years she had stuck with it, trying to make it work. She had convinced herself that a second divorce would destroy her family. When the time came, though, she had to admit that she was deeply unhappy. In 1979, she and Thomas Kitchens decided to divorce.

The reality of her books was no different from the reality of Judy Blume's life. She would confront divorce again, and it was difficult. But as she had written, it was not the end of the world.

With the end of the 1970s came a new era in American politics and social values. The 1980s saw Blume besieged by censors who criticized her for everything from sexual permissiveness to "lack of moral tone." Nonetheless, Blume retained her sense of humor.

Book Burnings

Controversy wasn't on my mind. I wanted only to write what I knew to be true. I wanted to write the best, the most honest books I could, the kinds of books I would have liked to read when I was younger. If someone had told me then I would become one of the most banned writers in America, I'd have laughed. [26]

—*Judy Blume*

JUDY BLUME WAS not going to leave New Mexico right away. Even though she and Thomas Kitchens were divorced in 1979, she felt that she needed to give her son Larry, then in high school, some stability. In six years, her children had attended six different schools, though at this point Randy had started college. As a compromise, Blume visited the East Coast often and maintained an apartment in New York City. At this point in her career, she had sold enough books to support herself and her children. "I learned that you can't expect another person to change your life," said Blume of this time period. "You have to make those changes yourself. I learned that there are worse things in life than living without a spouse." [27] For the time being, she would stay single and independent.

Coming out of an incredibly productive period of writing, Blume was having trouble moving on to her next book. She decided to rent an office for writing. The office was over a bakery, though, and she soon found the aroma of baked goods distracted her from writing. "Every day at noon I would rush downstairs to buy two glazed donuts and by three o'clock I would crave another round," remembers Blume. "After a few months and a few pounds I moved home again." [28]

For years, letters from young fans begged her to write a sequel to *Tales of a Fourth Grade Nothing*, but she couldn't think of an idea. "I remember exactly where I was when the idea finally came to me—in the shower, covered with soap and shampoo," she said. "And the idea seemed so simple I couldn't believe it had taken seven years. I would give the Hatchers a new baby." [29]

Superfudge finally emerged in 1980. In the second installment of the lively and comic Hatcher family saga, Peter Hatcher discovers that besides his younger brother, Fudge, stealing the show, he has new problems to contend with—his mother is having a baby and the family is leaving New York to move to Princeton, New Jersey, for a year. In addition to the old theme of feeling second-best, the book is about the added anxieties of starting over. Moving, too, had become a recurring theme in Blume's books, reflecting her own lifestyle. With its memorable scenes like the one where Fudge pastes the new baby with postage stamps, *Superfudge* was even more adored than *Tales of a Fourth Grade Nothing* and it sold a quarter of a million copies in its first four months, going on to win dozens of readers' choice awards.

The following year, Blume returned to her young-adult audience and released a book that captured some of her experience in New Mexico. Initially, the idea for *Tiger Eyes* came about when a group of producers approached Blume and asked her to write a screenplay for a television movie. She came up with the story, but the producers rejected it, telling her it wasn't a "Judy Blume story." Blume was hurt, but she stood by her original idea. She sat down and converted the script into a novel.

Tiger Eyes is about a teenager, Davey, whose father is killed in a hold-up of the Atlantic City, New Jersey, 7-Eleven convenience store he runs. Devastated, her mother takes Davey and her younger brother on a trip to New Mexico to visit some relatives, and they decide to stay there indefinitely while the family mourns. Davey, through the help of a new friend, begins to cope with some of her feelings, and at the book's resolution, starts to heal.

Tiger Eyes captures the fear, anger, and sorrow in suddenly losing a father, and Blume revisited the painful year of her father's death while writing about Davey. With its themes of violence and death, it was also her most serious book to date. The *New York Times* called the book "masterly" and *Tiger Eyes* was nominated for an American Book Award. When they saw the success of her book, television producers returned and asked her to turn *Tiger Eyes* into a screenplay, which she did in collaboration with another writer. While the novel is considered Judy Blume's finest work, to this day, a film version of *Tiger Eyes* has not been made. Blume has said that she hopes Larry, now a filmmaker, will help her make the movie someday.

Something else was happening to Blume in the early 1980s. For every letter she received from a devoted fan, she received a complaint about her books—and worse, threats from parents and teachers. For some years, she had encountered people who questioned her work, particularly some of her content about masturbation and puberty.

"I remember the night a woman phoned," recalled Blume of a particular incident, "asking if I had written *Are You There God? It's Me, Margaret.* When I replied that I had, she called me a Communist and slammed down the phone. I never did figure out if she equated Communism with menstruation or religion, the two major concerns in twelve-year-old Margaret's life." [30]

In the late 1970s, Blume had heard anecdotes about people who were offended by her books. There was a mother of a thirteen-year-old boy who cut out two pages describing a wet dream in *Then Again, Maybe I Won't.* There was also a librarian who took *Deenie* off the shelf because it discussed masturbation. The school's principal had told the librarian, "It would be different if Deenie was a boy. That would be normal." [31] In the beginning, these incidents seemed few and far between. It didn't occur to Blume that these were more than isolated instances or that her books would be reinterpreted over the years.

Now, though, a new generation of infuriated adults began to descend upon her work. The beginning of the decade brought a turn toward more conservative, family values—a contrast to the 1970s' celebration of feminism and personal freedom. Groups like the Moral Majority and the Eagle Forum as well as the National Association of Christian Educators took advantage of a sympathetic White House to gain newfound power, enabling them to ban and restrict any literature they saw as a threat to their beliefs. "It all began in 1980," Blume recalls.

"Literally the day after Reagan was elected, the censors crawled out of the woodwork and nothing was the same."[32]

In the 1980s, book banning reached an all-time high, nearly tripling in frequency since the previous decade. Blume became public enemy number one to book banners, a title that she still holds today. Some activists have even written and distributed pamphlets such as "How to Rid Your Schools and Library of Judy Blume Books." The most contested of her books have been *Deenie*; *Forever*; *Blubber*; and *Then Again, Maybe I Won't*, though some schools and libraries have banned all of Blume's books with no regard for their content but simply because the author was Judy Blume.

What teachers and parents have mainly taken issue with is the language and sexual subject matter in Blume's books. "Sexual" subject matter has been used loosely to include any discussion of puberty. *Then Again, Maybe I Won't* was challenged for its use of language and portrayal of puberty. *Deenie* has been challenged because of the passage about masturbation. *Forever* has been challenged because of its discussion of premarital sex and birth control—some have even gone so far as to label it pornography. But *Blubber* was challenged for a "lack of moral tone," specifically, the fact that the book's bullies are never punished for their wrong-doing. In that case, it was not what Blume wrote but what she didn't write that got her book banned.

Conservatives are not the only ones who have attacked Blume's books. Feminists have found fault with what they perceive as Judy Blume's traditional values and female characters who appear to be oblivious to the women's

> **Did you know...**
>
> It has been estimated that Judy Blume is the second most frequently challenged and banned American author behind only John Steinbeck.

movement. Others taking a politically correct approach have claimed that her works are racist and don't contain enough representation of non-white characters.

From either end, it seemed that Judy Blume could do no right. Even *Superfudge* was challenged for a reference to adultery. Remembering her own struggle to read *A Rage to Live* and watching some of her other peers battling similar reactions to their work, Blume began to feel angry about censorship. "Censors don't want children exposed to ideas different from their own," said Blume. "If every individual with an agenda had his/her way, the shelves in the school library would be close to empty." [33]

The censorship battle over Blume's books began to affect how her editors viewed her work. While her editors had always been supportive of whatever Blume wrote, once the controversy around her work exploded, they began to suggest that she eliminate potentially offensive passages from her writing. "My worst moment came when I was working with my editor on the manuscript of *Tiger Eyes*," she recalled. "When we came to the scene in which Davey allows herself to *feel* again after months of numbness following her father's death, I saw that a few lines alluding to masturbation had been circled. My editor put down his pencil and faced me. 'We want this book to reach as many readers as possible, don't we?' he asked." [34]

Among her legions of fans, there have been readers, parents, and teachers who have supported Judy Blume and have testified to the value of her work. Her favorite story is of a sixth grader in Colorado who petitioned to keep Judy Blume books in her school library and even went before her district school board to declare their importance to young people. The school board was moved by her plea and voted unanimously to keep the books available with no restrictions.

Still, Blume has watched censorship grow worse over the

years. She has since become a staunch advocate for freedom of speech. As a spokeswoman for the National Coalition Against Censorship, she has voiced her belief that book banning is destructive both for readers and writers. In the late 1990s, when J.K. Rowling's Harry Potter books came under fire for their magical content—which some readers interpreted as promoting occult or Satanic behavior—Blume was among Rowling's most vocal defenders. She wrote an editorial in the *New York Times*, urging book banners to lay off the Harry Potter books. She also edited a volume of writing by other censored authors called *Places I Never Meant To Be* in 1999. Any book that was banned, she reasoned, was just one more step toward total censorship.

"I believe that censorship grows out of fear, and because fear is contagious, some parents are easily swayed," said Blume. "Book banning satisfies their need to feel in control of their children's lives. This fear is often disguised as moral outrage. They want to believe that if their children don't read about it, their children won't know about it. And if they don't know about it, it won't happen." [35]

In order to address the problem of censorship in a deeper way, Judy Blume decided to use her wealth to establish The Kids Fund in 1981. The Kids Fund uses proceeds from her books to benefit organizations all over the country that encourage dialogue between children and adults. By helping to open communication between generations, Blume hoped that parents would be less afraid and more capable of understanding their children. If parents could see that their children were only looking for answers and not looking to get into trouble, perhaps they would feel more comfortable with books that told them the truth.

Judy Blume's more recent writings have shown her range as an author and have given something important back to her many readers and fans. Books like Smart Women *dealt with complex emotional issues from an adult perspective, while* Letters to Judy *let Blume respond publicly to some of the many letters she has received throughout her career.*

Family Business

There is no such thing as perfection in family life, as much as we might wish for it. We do the best we can and hope it will all work out. [36]

—*Judy Blume*

IN 1983, JUDY Blume was defending the social worth of her books against censors, but the truth was that she held family values as dear as the people who claimed she was trying to destroy them. Still plagued by the effects of divorce, she released a second adult book, *Smart Women*. In this novel, Margo and B.B. are two divorced women with teenage daughters. Then, B.B.'s ex-husband moves in next door to Margo, and they soon fall in love, putting a strain on the women's friendship. The daughters, too, react to the difficult situation, acting out their frustration and anger.

Like *Wifey*, *Smart Women* is about divorce, but it is also about what it is like to fall in love again as a middle-aged person. Blume wrote the book for adults but also for older teenagers who were looking to understand divorce from their parents' point of view. "I had always taken the children's side, because kids have so little control over their lives," she told Don Swaim. This time, however, she was trying to stay true to the parents' experience. But even while she was trying to present an adult perspective, critics remarked that Blume's portrayal of children in *Smart Women* was remarkably sensitive. While *Wifey* had earned something of a dubious reputation for its treatment of extramarital affairs, *Smart Women* was immediately embraced by adult readers.

Even while she was reaching out to adults, Judy Blume was getting back in touch with the girl of her youth by taking up a new hobby: tap dancing. "I tap danced six days a week," said Blume of her pursuit. "I went to this wonderful class, which was all professionals and young hopefuls and a couple of people like me. Oh, there was this fantasy, my fantasy of being up on the stage in a Broadway musical." [37]

In 1984, the lure of the East Coast brought Blume back to New York City full time. She also returned to an old story. The picture book called *The Pain and the Great One* had its roots nearly fifteen years earlier when Blume's children were much younger:

> One rainy afternoon, when my children were about six and eight, and the house was filled with their friends, I suddenly got an idea. I sat right down and wrote this story. The brother and sister in this book are based on my daughter Randy and son Larry. The cat is

our first family pet. Originally published as a poem in *Free to Be You and Me*, it later became an illustrated picture book. It's my favorite of anything I've written for young children. Randy and Larry, who are grown now, still sometimes refer to each other as "The Pain" and "The Great One." [38]

Family and its intricate connections was still at the heart of everything Blume wrote.

By the mid-1980s, 35 million copies of her books were in print and Blume's popularity had reached staggering new heights. Her work was being translated and packaged into foreign editions on a regular basis all over Europe, Asia, and Israel. Still, she remained humble and often remarked that she wasn't quite sure how she had become so successful.

Undeterred by her wealth and success, Blume continued to correspond with her readers by mail, responding personally to as many letters as she could. "I have a wonderful, intimate relationship with kids. It's rare and lovely. They feel that they know me and that I know them," she told *Publishers Weekly*. Though she had gotten thousands of letters over the years from her readers, one letter in particular gave her an idea. A ten-year-old girl named Amy wrote to ask if Blume would write a book for adults that explained kids' problems.

Blume decided that the kids themselves could explain their problems better than she could. She began to compile some of her letters from young readers into a book called *Letters to Judy: What Your Kids Wish They Could Tell You*. Published in 1986, and two-and-a-half years in the making, the non-fiction *Letters to Judy* was unique among Blume's works. The purpose of the book would be exactly as Amy had imagined: to illustrate what kids were thinking and feeling about difficult issues they were afraid to discuss with their parents. "Why do kids confide in me? I've been trying to figure that out for years," she wrote in the book's introduction. "I'm still not sure I understand completely, but I know it's often easier to confide in someone you don't have to face at the breakfast table the next morning, someone who can't use anything you have to say against you."

The book is divided into sections about various topics such as divorce, bullying, sex, and puberty. These were the topics she had so often written about, and many of the letters she received were about the same issues. But there were also letters about runaways, suicide, and drug use, topics which Blume had not written about. Blume sifted through her letters and pulled out the most common themes, changing names and details, and even writing composites of several different letters. In each chapter, she responds to the letters, sharing experiences from her own life, and advising kids and parents how to deal with difficult matters. Acknowledging that she is not a professional counselor, Blume urges parents to read the book and assures them that her own children might need to talk to someone else, too. The important thing, asserted Blume, was to open the lines of honest communication. The back of the book lists resources for every problem described in the book, from hotline numbers to community support groups. All the proceeds of the book's sales would benefit the Kids Fund.

Soon after it was published, Blume learned that the book was indeed fulfilling its purpose. A mother of two teenagers wrote to tell her how *Letters to Judy* had opened a channel of communication between her and her children:

> She said that she was home fixing dinner, and her daughter was sitting in the kitchen, as kids and mothers do. She was reading from the book, and suddenly she started to cry—this is the daughter. And the mother turned around and said, "What is it?"

Her daughter started to read to her from the book. It was actually Laura's story—it touched off something about her own feelings. And the mother said, for the first time—in *years*—they sat down together—it's very sad, and it made me cry . . . And because of those letters they started to talk, the daughter opened up to her, and shared some feelings. That was very nice.[39]

Still, during the same interview, Blume asserted that *Letters to Judy* would most likely be her only work of nonfiction, not because she didn't enjoy the experience of writing it, but because she saw herself as a storyteller and not a writer preaching a message.

Meanwhile, her personal life again began to thrive. Blume had met a new man, a law professor and nonfiction writer named George Cooper, and fell in love for the third time. Having learned from her mistakes, Blume had chosen a mate this time that she would stay with. This was also the beginning of a third phase of family life for Judy Blume. Cooper had a young teenage daughter, Amanda, from a previous marriage. Blume and Cooper moved into an apartment in New York City together, and Amanda would stay with them a few months out of the year. Judy's children Randy and Larry were away at college at this time. They were wary at first about their mother's new relationship, but they soon grew to accept it. For her part, Amanda was thrilled that her father had become romantically involved with the famous writer.

In 1987, Blume and Cooper were married in an informal ceremony on the balcony of their New York City apartment. Blume's mother

Did you know...

In 1983, Judy Blume received the Eleanor Roosevelt Humanitarian Award in recognition of her altruistic work with Kids Fund.

was hospitalized a few months later with pneumonia. It had been her wish to see Blume married again, and she was thankful that her mother had made it to the ceremony. She died shortly thereafter.

After the wedding, Blume and Cooper moved to Connecticut, where her next few books would be set. In fact, many of the characters in her next book, *Just as Long as We're Together,* would be named for stores in the town of Westport where Blume and Cooper were fixing up an old house.

Just as Long as We're Together marked Blume's return to her young-adult audience, presenting a trio of young girls who would, like the Hatcher family, become recurring characters. Yet another book about divorce, *Just as Long* broaches the subject in a more contemporary manner than *It's Not the End of the World*. Thirteen-year-old Stephanie's parents are getting a separation, but they do so quietly and secretly. Stephanie's mother works and makes a good living, so supporting her children is not a question. Still, Stephanie has to learn to live with seeing her father only once in a while as opposed to every day. When he comes for a visit she is happy to see him, but things are different. Says Stephanie in the book, "I don't know why but I suddenly felt shy. I guess it's because I'm a different person now, different than when dad left. I hadn't even started seventh grade then. Now, I'm almost a teenager." [*Just as Long*, p. 121]

Stephanie begins overeating to cope with her feelings. Her weight gain soon attracts cruel attention from her classmates who start calling her names. In the meantime, she is juggling her relationships with two best friends, Alison and Rachel, both of whom are vying for her attention. Over the course of the book, Stephanie learns to manage her feelings about her parents as well as her own behaviors. In contrast to the ending of *It's Not the End of the World*, there is a suggestion at the book's conclusion that Stephanie's parents may actually get back together.

The book was easy to write for Blume, who'd conjured up her young characters years before. Her initial plan was to write a trilogy with the first book about Stephanie, the second about Alison, and the third about Rachel. Still, it was missing a title. "My agent, Claire Smith, and I met for a lunch that lasted well into the afternoon," remembered Blume. "Finally, we resorted to singing old camp songs, trying to find a good title. Eventually, we decided on a line from the song 'Side by Side.'" [40]

Just as Long as We're Together was also marked by personal tragedy. When Judy Blume began writing the book, the college-age son of a good friend became ill with leukemia. When she was finished, he was very ill and Judy decided to dedicate the book to him. By the time it was published, he had died.

Blume was increasingly looking for new ways to help children. After the success of *Letters to Judy*, a second fundraising project was developed in 1988 with *The Judy Blume Memory Book*. The book, intended for Blume's young fans, was constructed as a type of journal. It left space for children to record their earliest memories, and it included quotes from several of Blume's books. The proceeds for *The Judy Blume Memory Book* went to fund a nonprofit organization that helped victims of child abuse. If her books were not helping families, her charitable actions certainly were.

Within the space of five years, Blume's life had changed dramatically. She had remarried, moved yet again into a new home, and had completed a new set of accomplishments, including her first—and likely, last—work of nonfiction. She had strengthened the family bonds of strangers, and she had built a new, stronger family of her own.

Here, Blume addresses the media at a press conference in New York in June 2002. New York State Education Commissioner Richard Mills was denounced for engaging in censorship on the statewide English Language Arts exam that is required for public high school students in New York.

8

Staying Young

I'm sixty-four years old, but I feel terribly young inside. [41]
—*Judy Blume*

BY THE 1990S, Judy Blume was getting to an age where some people consider retirement but she was still going strong, rolling out a steady stream of books. She and George Cooper were dividing their time between homes in Key West, Martha's Vineyard, and New York City. George Cooper was turning his own legal expertise into nonfiction crime books. The pair also kept busy with outdoor activities like hiking and kayaking. If Blume was aging, her youthful spirit had not been quelled.

In fact, Blume was as connected to her younger readers as she'd always been. During a summer vacation in Maine, she had a flash of inspiration imagining Sheila Tubman on an outdoor swing. She had just finished making the film adaptation of *Otherwise Known as Sheila the Great* with her son directing. She realized that she missed the character of Sheila Tubman and wanted to write about her again. The image of Sheila on the swing prompted Judy to return to the Hatcher family in *Fudge-a-Mania.* In the third Fudge book, Fudge develops a crush on Sheila Tubman, who is still Peter's nemesis. Luckily for Fudge and unluckily for Peter, the Hatchers decide to rent a summer house next door to the Tubman's. The setting of *Fudge-a-Mania* was derived from Blume's own vacation experience.

The book, as the other Fudge books had before it, came quickly and easily for Blume. She said of the series, "The thing about funny books is, they have to spill out spontaneously, or they don't work (at least that's how it is with me). Unlike a novel, which can take me three years and up to twenty drafts, Fudge books either come or they don't. Maybe that's also why I write so few of them." [42] Still, at the time Blume thought she'd had it with the Hatchers and that *Fudge-a-Mania* would be her final Fudge book.

It had become customary for Blume to shift gears between books and this meant choosing a different tone and audience for her next work. After *Fudge-a-Mania*, Blume returned to her young characters from *Just as Long as We're Together.* Blume had tried to develop a television series based on that book's three main characters, but it never came to pass. But they still were very much in her mind, so she devoted a whole novel to the character Rachel Robinson called *Here's to You, Rachel Robinson.* "Rachel's character was inspired by a friend of mine when I was in junior high, a high achieving perfectionist," explained Blume. "Also, I once received a letter from a twelve-year-old who was taking college courses. Because she was intellectually ahead of her twelve-year-old friends, they didn't want to be her friends anymore. She confided that she'd give it all up just to be a normal girl." [43]

In *Here's to You, Rachel Robinson*, Rachel is an over-achiever who feels as though she is invisible while her older brother Charles makes waves in the family with his rebellious behavior. Says Rachel in the book, "Trouble in our family is spelled with a capital C and has been as long as I can remember. The C stands for Charles. He's my older brother, two years and four months older to be exact. Ever since the phone call about him last night, I've felt incredibly tense. And now, at this very minute, my parents are driving up to Vermont, to Charles' boarding school, to find out if he's actually been kicked out or if he's just been suspended again." [*Here's to You*, p. 1]

Charles' return home adds to Rachel's list of stresses, which include trying to keep her record of straight A's, practicing the flute, becoming a Natural Helper in school, having crushes on boys, and negotiating her friendships with Stephanie and Alison. But through her brother, Rachel learns how to be a little less perfect. *Here's to You* was both comic and serious, a glimpse at middle-school life and sibling rivalry. For fans of *Just as Long as We're Together*, it was a satisfying follow-up.

Blume's next book, her third for adults, followed. *Summer Sisters* had been in development for several years, long before Blume actually sat down to start writing it. The book's basic idea came on a summer vacation in Martha's Vineyard:

Every afternoon I'd row the dinghy around the pond, often out to the jetty where it opens to the Sound. Alone on the water, with time to think, the idea for *Summer Sisters* first came to me. It was just a vague idea then—two young women from very different families in Santa Fe spend a series of summers on the Vineyard, one the guest of the other's family. That was it. No more. The idea stayed in my head for ten years before I actually began to write anything down. For a long time I thought of the book as Caitlin Summers and I thought the characters might go from age twelve to maybe seventeen. I never guessed it would take almost twenty years to tell their story or that so many adult characters would be involved, jumping in and telling the story from their points of view. [44]

Eventually, Blume and Cooper would buy their own house on Martha's Vineyard on the same lake where they'd vacationed. In 1993, Blume turned one of the small cabins on their property into a writing studio and set out to work on the novel. The story follows two women, Caitlin and Vix, from their teenage years spent on Martha's Vineyard to their adulthood and examines some of the complications of their friendship created by their relationships with men.

The book would go through several drafts, the last of which was completed in 1997. It was by far Blume's most difficult book to write. *Summer Sisters* proved to be a challenge because it fell in between Blume's other works. The story itself was about young adults and dealt with many of the themes Blume had examined in her books for younger readers, but at the same time *Summer Sisters*

> **Did you know...**
>
> In 1996, the Young Adult Library Services Association of the American Library Association presented Judy Blume with the Margaret A. Edwards Award for Outstanding Literature for Young Adults, which is awarded for lifetime achievement in writing for teenagers.

was intended for a more mature audience. It made for a tricky balancing act. Furthermore, Blume had spent so much time thinking about her characters that she couldn't get them out of her head and onto the page. "I call it my book from hell," Blume told an interviewer from *Bookpage*. "This book was very tough to get right because these two young women were on my mind for a long time." Blume has said that somewhere in between her multiple drafts she considered giving the whole thing up and burning the manuscript.

By the time she completed her last rewrite, however, the book had taken on a whole new life with a set of characters Blume had not previously imagined. "Last summer, on my very last re-write of twenty re-writes, the men's voices came into it for the first time," said Blume. "I let Sharkey, Daniel, Gus and Bru talk. I realized that we were getting a whole other view of Caitlin. *Summer Sisters* is really her story, but we can't know anything about her, because she doesn't let us, except through other characters. That's when it started to happen." [45]

Blume was convinced that *Summer Sisters* would end her career—that readers and critics would hate the book and give up on her. She begged Cooper to buy the book back from the publisher before it hit stores. But Blume's fears were unfounded and she was rewarded for her hard work. *Summer Sisters* captured the attention of an enthusiastic readership and made it to number one on the *New York Times* best-seller list.

In the meantime, Blume's daughter Randy had become a published author in her own right with a novel based on her experiences as a commercial airline pilot, *Crazy in the Cockpit*. The book was dedicated to her mother.

And then Fudge—who had so often come back to surprise everyone, including his creator—took on a new presence as the subject of a Saturday morning television show from

1996–1998. The series was capped off by a two-hour adaptation of *Fudge-a-Mania*. The experience was a mixed one, and Blume would ultimately be disappointed with the way the television show was handled.

Fortunately, the show was not the end of the Hatcher family. Blume was reuniting them for a fourth installment, thirty years after the release of their debut, *Tales of a Fourth Grade Nothing*. Just as *Tales* was inspired by her son, *Double Fudge* was inspired by Blume's grandson. "Elliot invented a game when he was little where I had to play the part of Fudge and he got to be Peter. It drove the rest of the family crazy," Blume says. "He kept asking for another Fudge book, and I always said I'd do it if I got an idea." [46]

Blume got an idea. In *Double Fudge*, Peter, now in seventh grade, and five-year-old Fudge travel with their parents to Washington, D.C., where they unexpectedly meet up with relatives from Hawaii. One of the cousins, it turns out, shares Fudge's name, which gives everyone cause for alarm. Later, the whole strange clan ends up coming to visit the Hatchers in New York with laughably silly results.

Though they are popular as ever, Blume feels that the Fudge books have evolved over time. "There's certainly a difference to me between *Tales of a Fourth Grade Nothing* and this book," Blume said. "The first one was much more cartoony. With *Superfudge*, the tone became more realistic, especially when it came to the family." [47] Perhaps it is because they are so realistic that the Hatchers refuse to stay quiet.

Blume's influence on a generation was also being felt and acknowledged by grateful adults who had grown up with her memorable stories. In 1998, a performance group in Chicago called Annoyance Theater staged a tribute called "What Every Girl Should Know...An Ode to Judy Blume," comically uniting Margaret, Deenie, and Katharine onstage.

By the turn of the millennium, many of Judy Blume's first readers had grown up. It was not unusual for her to be approached by a young mother who wanted Blume to sign an original copy of *Are You There God? It's Me, Margaret* or *Then Again, Maybe I Won't* for her children. Blume's books had spanned one generation and were filtering down to the next one.

Though for years she had toyed with the idea of giving up writing, Blume herself made no plans to sit still. There were still more ideas to explore and more feelings to convey. If the success of *Summer Sisters* taught her anything it was that new frontiers are worth crossing.

> For me, writing has its ups and downs. After I had written more than ten books I thought seriously about quitting. I felt I couldn't take the loneliness anymore. I thought I would rather be anything than a writer. But I've finally come to appreciate the freedom of writing. I accept the fact that it's hard and solitary work. And I worry about running out of ideas or repeating myself. So I'm always looking for new challenges. [48]

Ever humble, Blume attributes her phenomenal success to her dedicated fans. "Everything I have today is because of my readers. We have something to give each other. There's a connection, you know, and it's so sweet." [49]

Humanitarian and champion of free speech, Blume has used her writing to better the world, to break barriers, and open up dialogue. She has entertained and educated millions of readers. Most importantly, Judy Blume continues to tell true stories. She may have grown older but she has not lost her connection to the young girl inside herself, or, for that matter, her audience.

1   Educational Paperback Association,
    http://www.edupaperback.org/authorbios/Blume_Judy.html

2   Marcus, Leonard S., ed. *Author Talk*. New York: Simon & Schuster,
    2000, p. 6

3   Weidt, Maryann. *Presenting Judy Blume*. Twayne, 1989, p. 4

4   Author Studies, Scholastic books. *http://www2.scholastic.com/teachers/
    authorsandbooks/authorstudies*

5   Educational Paperback Association

6   *www.judyblume.com*

7   Marcus, p. 4

8   Ibid., p. 5

9   Blume, Judy. *Letters to Judy: What Your Kids Wish They Could Tell
    You*. New York: Putnam, 1986, p. 58

10 Ibid., p. 58

11 *www.judyblume.com*

12 Weidt, p. 4

13 Eaglen, Audrey. "Answers From Blume Country: An Interview with
    Judy Blume." *Top of the News*, p. 233

14 Weidt, p. 54

15 Ibid., p. 58

16 *www.judyblume.com*

17 Ibid

18 Weidt, pp. 80–81

19 *www.judyblume.com*

20 *Letters to Judy*, p. 45

21 *www.judyblume.com*

22 Steinberg, Sybil. "PW Interviews: Judy Blume." *Publishers Weekly*,
    April 17, 1978, pp. 6–7

23 Dorfman, Alison. "Alison Dorfman Interviews Judy Blume."
    Boldtype, June 1998
    http://www.randomhouse.com/boldtype/0698/blume/interview.html

24 Ibid

25 *www.judyblume.com*

26 Blume, Judy, ed. *Places I Never Meant To Be*. New York: Simon &
    Schuster, 1999

27 *Letters to Judy*, p. 124

28 *www.judyblume.com*

29 Ibid

30 Ibid

31 *Places I Never Meant To Be*

32 Mackler, Carolyn. "Judy Blume on Sex, the Suburbs, and Summer Sisters." *Ms.*, July/August 1998, pp. 89–90

33 *www.judyblume.com*

34 *Places I Never Meant To Be*

35 *www.judyblume.com*

36 *Letters to Judy*, p. 31

37 "Starring Judy Blume as Herself." *www.Gurl.com*

38 *www.judyblume.com*

39 Marley, Kate. "Letters to Judy: An Interview with Judy Blume." *Baltimore's Child*, July/August 1986

40 *www.judyblume.com*

41 Grossman, Mary Ann. "Blume Doesn't Sound Too Convincing When She Talks About Retiring." Knight Ridder/Tribune News Service, October 9, 2002 pK7

42 *www.judyblume.com*

43 Ibid

44 Ibid

45 *randomhouse.com*

46 *randomhouse.com*

47 Grossman, pK7

48 *www.judyblume.com*

49 Kanner, Ellen. "A Woman for all Seasons Reflects on Growing Up and Growing Older." *Bookpage*, May 1999

1938 Judy Sussman born in Elizabeth, New Jersey.

1959 Judy Sussman marries John Blume.

1961 Blume's daughter, Randy, is born.

1963 Blume's son, Larry, is born.

1969 *The One in the Middle Is the Green Kangaroo* published.

1970 *Iggie's House* published.
Are You There God? It's Me, Margaret published.
Blume makes the *New York Times* Best Books for Children list.

1971 *Then Again, Maybe I Won't* published.
Freckle Juice published.

1972 *Tales of a Fourth Grade Nothing* published.
Otherwise Known as Sheila the Great published.
It's Not the End of the World published.

1973 *Deenie* published.

1974 *Blubber* published.

1975 *Forever* published.
Blume divorces John Blume.
Blume marries Thomas Kitchens.

1977 *Starring Sally J. Freedman as Herself* published.

1978 *Wifey* published.
Forever adapted into a movie.

1979 Blume divorces Thomas Kitchens.

1980 *Superfudge* published.

1981 *Tiger Eyes* published.

1983 Blume wins the Eleanor Roosevelt Humanitarian Award.
Smart Women published.

1984 *The Pain and the Great One* published.

1986 *Letters to Judy: What Your Kids Wish They Could Tell You* published.

1987 *Freckle Juice* adapted into an animated movie.
Just as Long as We're Together published.
Blume marries George Cooper.

1990 *Fudge-a-Mania* published.

1993 *Here's to You, Rachel Robinson* published.

1996 Fudge book series adapted for television.
Blume wins the Margaret A. Edwards Award.

1999 *Summer Sisters* published.

2002 *Double Fudge* published.

ARE YOU THERE GOD? IT'S ME, MARGARET

Twelve-year-old Margaret, who is half-Jewish, half-Christian, has just moved to a new town where she makes friends with a group of girls who discuss bras, their periods, and boys in school. Filled with anxiety about all these changes, Margaret prays that her body will develop and she will be a normal teenager.

BLUBBER

Jill watches on with some amusement as classroom bullies torment an overweight student, until the same bullies turn on her.

SUPERFUDGE

Twelve-year-old Peter Hatcher already loathes the fuss his younger brother Fudge causes, but now he has learned that his mother is having another baby and the whole family will be moving to Princeton, New Jersey.

TIGER EYES

Davey is a young teenager when her father is killed in a holdup, and her family consequently moves to New Mexico to mourn his passing. Besides coming to terms with his death, Davey must learn how to care for her mother and sort through the conflicting messages from the adults around her.

THE ONE IN THE MIDDLE IS THE GREEN KANGAROO (Bradbury Press, 1969)

IGGIE'S HOUSE (Bradbury, 1970)

ARE YOU THERE GOD? IT'S ME, MARGARET (Bradbury, 1970)

THEN AGAIN, MAYBE I WON'T (Bradbury, 1971)

FRECKLE JUICE (Four Winds Press, 1971)

IT'S NOT THE END OF THE WORLD (Bradbury, 1972)

TALES OF A FOURTH GRADE NOTHING (Dutton, 1972)

OTHERWISE KNOWN AS SHEILA THE GREAT (Dutton, 1972)

DEENIE (Bradbury, 1973)

BLUBBER (Bradbury, 1974)

FOREVER (Bradbury, 1975)

STARRING SALLY J. FREEDMAN AS HERSELF (Bradbury, 1977)

WIFEY (Putnam, 1978)

SUPERFUDGE (Dutton, 1980)

TIGER EYES (Bradbury, 1981)

THE JUDY BLUME DIARY (Dell, 1981)

SMART WOMEN (Putnam, 1983)

THE PAIN AND THE GREAT ONE (Bradbury, 1984)

LETTERS TO JUDY: WHAT YOUR KIDS WISH THEY COULD TELL YOU (Putnam, 1986)

JUST AS LONG AS WE'RE TOGETHER (Orchard Books, 1987)

FUDGE-A-MANIA (Dutton, 1990)

HERE'S TO YOU, RACHEL ROBINSON (Orchard, 1993)

SUMMER SISTERS (Delacorte Books, 1999)

PLACES I NEVER MEANT TO BE [Edited by Judy Blume] (Simon & Shuster, 1999)

DOUBLE FUDGE (Dutton, 2002)

FUDGE (*Tales of a Fourth Grade Nothing*, *Superfudge*, *Fudge-a-Mania*, and *Double Fudge*): The success of Blume's four Fudge books is largely due to the wacky young Farley Hatcher—Fudge for short. Fudge generally creates a comic nuisance, either by swallowing a turtle or by developing a crush on his brother's archenemy.

MARGARET (*Are You There God? It's Me, Margaret*): Margaret was the first preteen to utter a prayer for menstruation in literature, and her candor and poignant insecurity has made her an unforgettable Judy Blume personality.

SALLY J. FREEDMAN (*Starring Sally J. Freedman as Herself*): The heroine of Blume's only historical novel who imagines Hitler is alive and living in Florida, and enlists her whole family to perform in her plays, has an imaginative charm—most likely because she is Blume's most autobiographical character.

ARE YOU THERE, GOD? IT'S ME MARGARET: *New York Times* Best Books for Children List, 1970; Nene Award, 1975; Young Hoosier Book Award, 1976; North Dakota Children's Choice, 1979; Great Stone Face Award, New Hampshire Library Association, 1980

BLUBBER: Arizona Young Readers Award, 1977; Young Readers' Choice Award, Pacific Northwest Library Association, 1977; North Dakota Children's Choice Award, 1983; *New York Times* Outstanding Book of the Year, 1974

FRECKLE JUICE: Michigan Young Readers' Award, Michigan Council of Teachers, 1980

FUDGE-A-MANIA: California Young Reader Medal, 1993; Iowa Children's Choice Award, 1993; Nene Award from the Children of Hawaii, 1993; Nevada Young Readers' Award, Nevada Library Association, 1993; Sunshine State Young Readers' Award, Florida Association for Media in Education, 1993; Pennsylvania Young Readers' Choice Award, Pennsylvania School Librarians Association, 1993; Michigan Readers' Choice Award, Michigan Reading Association, 1993

HERE'S TO YOU, RACHEL ROBINSON: Parents' Choice Award, Parents' Choice Foundation, 1993

JUST AS LONG AS WE'RE TOGETHER: Young Readers' List, Virginia State Reading Association, 1989

OTHERWISE KNOWN AS SHEILA THE GREAT: South Carolina Children's Book Award, 1978

THE PAIN AND THE GREAT ONE: Young Readers' Choice Award, Alabama Library Association, 1986; Children's Choices, International Reading Association, and Children's Book Council Committee, 1985

SUPERFUDGE: Texas Bluebonnet Award, 1980; Michigan Young Readers' Award, 1981; International Reading Association Children's Choice Award, 1981; First Buckeye Children's Book Award, 1982; Nene Award, 1982; Sue Hefley Book Award, Louisiana Association of School Libraries, 1982; United States Army in Europe Kinderbuch Award, 1982; West Australian Young Readers' Book Award, 1982; North Dakota Children's Choice Award, 1982; Colorado Children's Book Award, 1982; Georgia Children's Book Award, 1982; Tennessee Children's Choice Award, 1982; Utah Children's Book Award, 1982; Northern Territory Young Readers' Award, 1983; Young Readers' Choice Award, Pacific Northwest Library Association, 1983; Garden State Children's Book Award, 1983; Iowa Children's Choice Award,

1983; Arizona Young Readers' Award, 1983; California Young Readers' Award, 1983; Young Hoosier Book Award, 1983

TALES OF A FOURTH GRADE NOTHING: Charlie May Swann Children's Book Award, 1972; Young Readers' Choice Award, Pacific Northwest Library Association, 1975; Sequoyah Children's Book Award of Oklahoma, 1975; Massachusetts Children's Book Award, 1977; Georgia Children's Book Award, 1977; South Carolina Children's Book Award, 1977; Rhode Island Library Association Award, 1978; North Dakota Children's Choice Award, 1980; West Australian Young Readers' Award, 1980; United States Army in Europe Kinderbuch Award, 1981; Great Stone Face, New Hampshire Library Council, 1981

TIGER EYES: American Book Award Nomination, 1983; Dorothy Canfield Fisher Children's Book Award, 1983; California Young Readers' Medal, 1983

Blume, Judy, ed. *Places I Never Meant To Be*. New York: Simon & Schuster, 1999.

Blume, Judy. *Letters to Judy: What Your Kids Wish They Could Tell You*. New York: Putnam, 1986.

Dorfman, Alison. "Alison Dorfman Interviews Judy Blume." *Boldtype*, June, 1998.
[http://www.randomhouse.com/boldtype/0698/blume/interview.html]

Eaglen, Audrey. "Answers From Blume Country: An Interview with Judy Blume." *Top of the News*, Spring 1978, pp. 233–43.

Educational Paperback Association,
[http://www.edupaperback.org/authorbios/Blume_Judy.html]

Francke, Linda Bird, with Lisa Whitman. "Growing Up with Judy." *Newsweek*, October 9, 1978, p. 99.

Grossman, Mary Ann. "Blume Doesn't Sound too Convincing When She Talks About Retiring. "Knight Ridder/Tribune News Service, October 9, 2002 pK7.

"Starring Judy Blume as Herself." www.Gurl.com
[www.judyblume.com]

Kanner, Ellen. "A Woman for all Seasons Reflects on Growing Up and Growing Older." *Bookpage,* May 1999. [www.bookpage.com]

Mackler, Carolyn. "Judy Blume on Sex, the Suburbs, and Summer Sisters." *Ms.*, July/August 1998, pp. 89–90.

Marcus, Leonard S., ed. *Author Talk*. New York: Simon & Schuster, 2000.

Marley, Kate. "Letters to Judy: An Interview with Judy Blume." *Baltimore's Child*, July/August 1986.

Teachers @ Random House.
[http://www.randomhouse.com/teachers/authors/blum.html]

Author Studies Homepage, Scholastic Books.
[http://www2.scholastic.com/teachers/authorsandbooks/authorstudies]

Steinberg, Sybil. "PW Interviews: Judy Blume." *Publishers Weekly*, April 17, 1978, pp. 6–7.

Swaim, Don. Interview with Judy Blume, CBS Radio, 1984.

Weidt, Maryann N. *Presenting Judy Blume*. Boston: G.K. Hall, 1990.

Author Studies Homepage, Scholastic Books.
[http://www2.scholastic.com/teachers/authorsandbooks/authorstudies]

Children's Literature Review. Gale, Volume 2, 1976; Volume 15, 1988.

Educational Paperback Association.
[http://www.edupaperback.org/authorbios/Blume_Judy.html]

Judy Blume's Home Base.
[www.judyblume.com]

Lee, Betsey. *Judy Blume's Story*. Dillon Press, 1981.

Marcus, Leonard S., ed. *Author Talk*. New York: Simon & Schuster, 2000.

Random House Authors.
[http://www.randomhouse.com/teachers/authors/blum.html]

"Starring Judy Blume as Herself." www.Gurl.com

Weidt, Maryann. *Presenting Judy Blume*. Twayne, 1989.

http://www.carr.lib.md.us/mae/blume/blume.htm
[Mona Kerby's The Author Corner]

http://www.edupaperback.org/authorbios/Blume_Judy.html
[Educational Paperback Association]

http://www.judyblume.com
[Judy Blume's Home Base]

http://www.judyblume.com/articles/NYPL_online_chat_11-24.02.html
[New York Public Library Online Chat]

http://www.randomhouse.com/teachers/authors/blum.html
[Random House Authors]

http://www2.scholastic.com/teachers/authorsandbooks/authorstudies.jhtml
[Author Studies Homepage, Scholastic Books]

ELISA LUDWIG studied literature and writing at Vassar College and Temple University. She is currently a freelance writer based in Philadelphia, contributing to a number of different publications including the *Philadelphia Inquirer* and the *Philadelphia Daily News*.